J   38749007814781H
523.46   Bloom, J. P., author.
BLO   Saturn

W9-AQK-674

Hickory Flat Public Library
2740 East Cherokee Drive
Canton, Georgia 30115

SEQUOYAH REGIONAL LIBRARY

3 8749 0078 14781

Saturn

by J.P. Bloom

PROPERTY OF
THE SEQUOYAH REGIONAL
LIBRARY SYSTEM CANTON, GA

ABDO
PLANETS
Kids

abdopublishing.com

Published by Abdo Kids, a division of ABDO, PO Box 398166, Minneapolis, Minnesota 55439.

Copyright © 2015 by Abdo Consulting Group, Inc. International copyrights reserved in all countries. No part of this book may be reproduced in any form without written permission from the publisher.

Printed in the United States of America, North Mankato, Minnesota.

102014

012015

THIS BOOK CONTAINS
RECYCLED MATERIALS

Photo Credits: NASA, Science Source, Shutterstock, Thinkstock

Production Contributors: Teddy Borth, Jennie Forsberg, Grace Hansen

Design Contributors: Candice Keimig, Laura Rask, Dorothy Toth

Library of Congress Control Number: 2014943790

Cataloging-in-Publication Data

J.P. Bloom.

 Saturn / J.P. Bloom.

  p. cm. -- (Planets)

ISBN 978-1-62970-720-4 (lib. bdg.)

Includes index.

1. Saturn (Planet)--Juvenile literature. 2. Solar system--Juvenile literature. I. Title.

523.46--dc23

2014943790

Table of Contents

Saturn

Saturn is a **planet**. Planets **orbit** stars. Planets in our solar system orbit the sun.

4

Saturn is the sixth

closest **planet** to the sun.

Saturn is 887 million miles

(1.2 billion km) from the sun.

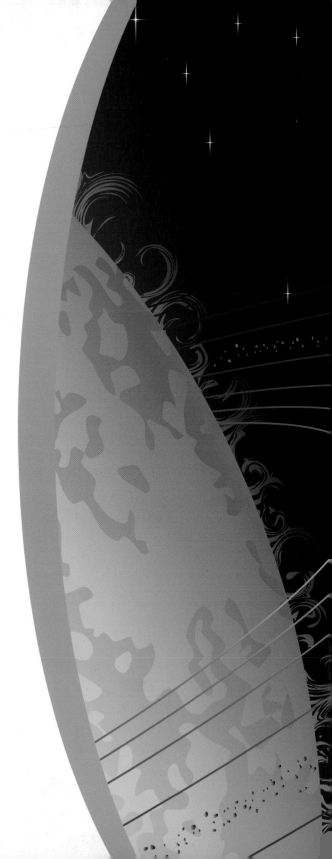

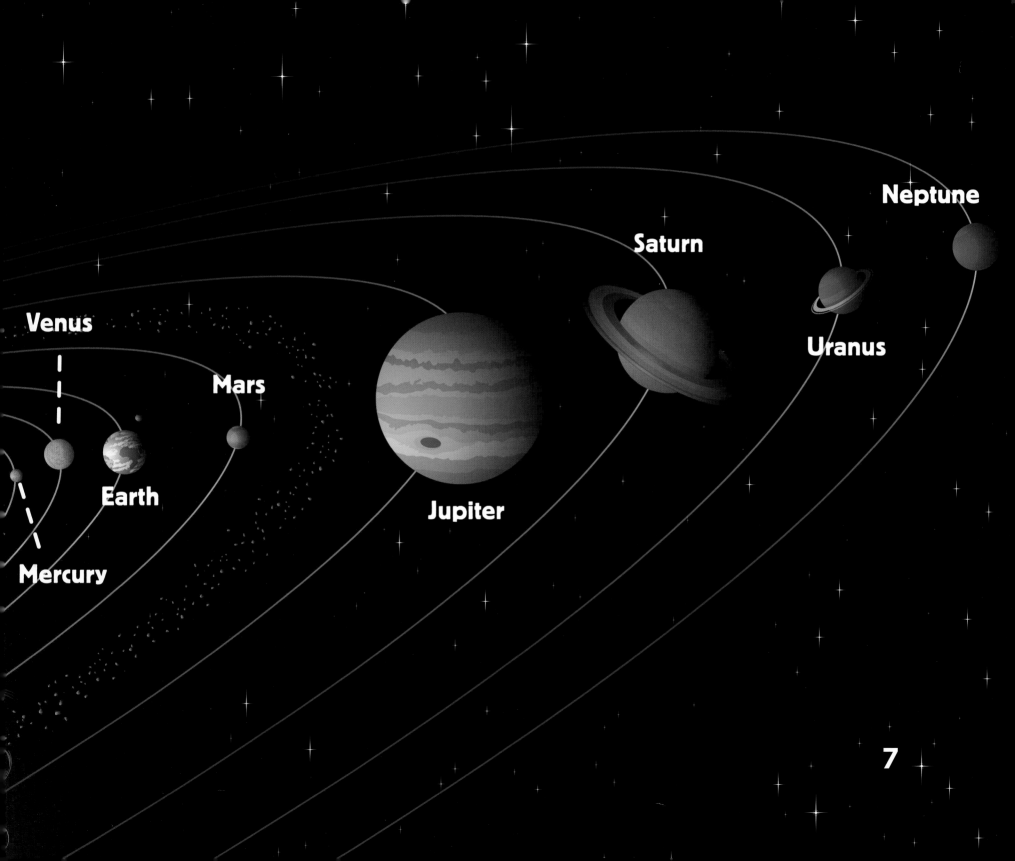

Venus

Mercury

Earth

Mars

Jupiter

Saturn

Uranus

Neptune

7

Saturn fully **orbits** the sun every 29 years. One year on Saturn is 29 years on Earth.

Earth

9

Saturn spins while in **orbit**.

One full spin takes about

11 hours. One day on

Saturn is 11 hours on Earth.

Titan
(moon)

Saturn is a giant ball of gas.

You cannot stand on Saturn.

Jupiter, Uranus, and Neptune
are also made of gases.

13

Saturn's Rings

Rings surround Saturn. The rings are made of rocks and ice. Some pieces are the size of dust. Others are as big as cars.

key

purple

most rocks
> 2 inches (5 cm)

green

most rocks
< 2 inches (5 cm)

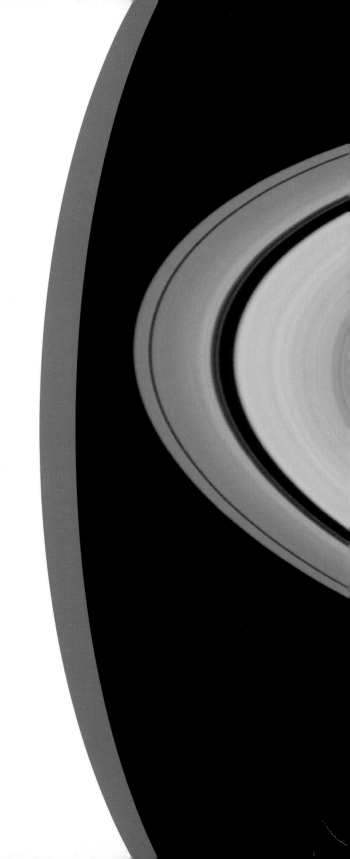

The rings **reflect** the sun's light.

This makes Saturn very colorful.

16

17

Saturn's Moons

Saturn has many moons. Scientists have counted over 60. Saturn's largest moon is Titan.

Janus

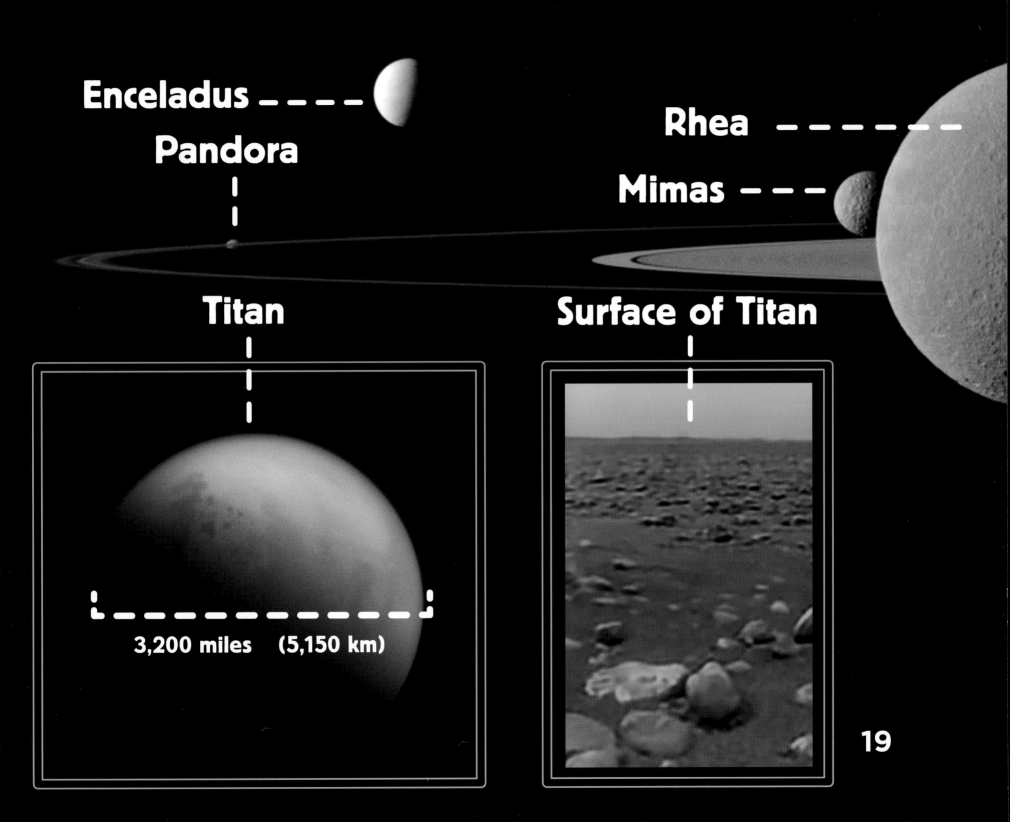

Enceladus - - - -

Pandora

Rhea - - - - - -

Mimas - - -

Titan

Surface of Titan

3,200 miles   (5,150 km)

19

Saturn from Earth

You can see Saturn from Earth on a clear night. You will not need a telescope!

20

– – – Saturn

21

More Facts

- Scientists think that Saturn's rings formed when one of its moons exploded.

- Sometimes large storms occur on Saturn. Winds on Saturn can reach very high speeds.

- The Pioneer 11 was the first spacecraft to fly by Saturn in 1979. It studied Saturn's rings and its largest moon, Titan.

Glossary

orbit – the path of a space object as it moves around another space object. To orbit is to follow this path.

planet – a large, round object in space (such as Earth) that travels around a star (such as the sun).

reflect – able to shine light back.

Index

abdokids.com

Use this code to log on to abdokids.com and access crafts, games, videos, and more!

Abdo Kids Code:
PSK7204